CW00350224

THE LITTLE BOOK OF

FRIENDSHIP

Parts of this book were first published in 2020 by Trigger, an imprint of Shaw Callaghan Ltd.

This expanded edition published in 2023 by OH! an Imprint of Welbeck Non-Fiction Limited, part of Welbeck Publishing Group. Based in London and Sydney.
www.welbeckpublishing.com

Compilation text © Welbeck Non-Fiction Limited 2023
Design © Welbeck Non-Fiction Limited 2023

Disclaimer:
OH! encourages diversity and different viewpoints. However, all views, thoughts, and opinions expressed in this book are not necessarily representative of Welbeck Publishing Group as an organization. All material in this book is set out in good faith for general guidance; no liability can be accepted for loss or expense incurred in following the information given. In particular, this book is not intended to replace expert medical or phychiatric advice. It is intended for informational purposes only and for your own personal use and guidance. It is not intended to diagnose, treat or act as a substitute for professional medical advice.

ISBN 978-1-80069-346-3

Original compilation: Trigger
Editorial: Victoria Denne
Design: Fusion Graphic Design Ltd
Project manager: Russell Porter
Production: Jess Brisley

A CIP catalogue record for this book is available from the British Library

Printed in China

10 9 8 7 6 5 4 3 2 1

THE LITTLE BOOK OF
FRIENDSHIP

FOR WHEN LIFE
GETS A LITTLE TOUGH

CONTENTS

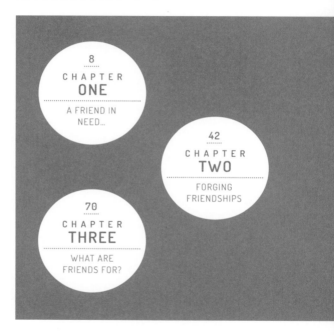

INTRODUCTION

Modern life can be filled with so much: from the daily commute, a hectic schedule, cooking an evening meal, to those crucial turning points: quitting your job, moving house, finding love. Between the noise, it can be hard to make and maintain friendships. *The Little Book of Friendship* offers a little guidance for when the scales of life are tipped, times are turbulent and a moment of companionship is needed. From the minds of some of the world's most well-known figures, learn to prioritize your friendships and truly value your loved ones, even when times are tough.

CHAPTER
1

WHAT ARE FRIENDS FOR?

What exactly friendship is is hard to define – but let's give it a go anyway...

Friendship is the wine of life.

Edward Young

Friendship at first sight, like love at first sight, is said to be the only truth.

Herman Melville

Without friends, no one would want to
live, even if he had all other goods.

Aristotle

One of the most beautiful qualities of
true friendship is to understand and
to be understood.

Seneca

The world is so empty if one thinks only of mountains, rivers and cities; but to know someone who thinks and feels with us ...

... this makes the earth for us an inhabited garden.

Goethe

Friends are the best to turn to when
you're having a rough day.

Justin Bieber

I have learned that to be with those
I like is enough.

Walt Whitman

HOW MANY FRIENDS DO YOU NEED?

British psychologist and anthropologist Robin Dunbar famously held that a person can only maintain about **150 connections** at one time.

This will include an inner circle of about **5 friends** along with circles of more casual friends and acquaintances.

There is nothing on this earth more to be
prized than true friendship.

Thomas Aquinas

Friendship is the only cement that
will ever hold the world together.

Woodrow Wilson

No man is an island.

John Donne

A good friend is like a four-leaf clover;
hard to find and lucky to have.

Irish proverb

My friends are my estate.

Emily Dickinson

I love my husband, but it is nothing like a conversation with a woman that understands you. I grow so much from those conversations.

Beyoncé

The better part of one's life consists
of his friendships.

Abraham Lincoln

A friend can tell you things you don't
want to tell yourself.

Frances Ward Weller

Friendship increases in visiting friends,
but in visiting them seldom.

Sir Francis Bacon

The feeling of friendship is like
that of being comfortably filled with
roast beef; love, like being enlivened
with champagne.

Samuel Johnson

Friendship improves happiness and abates misery, by the doubling of our joy and the dividing of our grief.

Cicero

A sweet friendship refreshes the soul.

Proverbs 27:9

What's helped me is having really good
friends I know I can rely on.

Drew Barrymore

Women's friendships are like a
renewable source of power.

Jane Fonda

I really believe you are the company you keep and you have to surround yourself with people who lift you up because the world knocks you down.

Maria Shriver

Truly great friends are hard to find,
difficult to leave, and impossible to forget.

G. Randolf

Rare as is true love, true friendship is rarer.

Jean de La Fontaine

A day without a friend is like a pot without a single drop of honey left inside.

Winnie-the-Pooh

A friend is one of the best things you can be and the greatest things you can have.

Sarah Valdez

Philia (φιλία) – friendship – is one of the four ancient Greek words for love. Plato believed that the combination of philia (friendship) and eros (romantic love) led to "friendship between lovers" – the highest form of love.

It is not a lack of love, but a lack of
friendship that makes unhappy marriages.

Friedrich Nietzsche

Friendship is the source of the greatest pleasures, and without friends even the most agreeable pursuits become tedious.

Thomas Aquinas

There is no happiness like that of being loved by your fellow creatures, and feeling that your presence is an addition to their comfort.

Charlotte Brontë

CHAPTER
2

FORGING FRIENDSHIPS

Making friends is easier said
than done, and yet, when
you find the right one, it's the
simplest thing in the world.

I don't like that man. I must get
to know him better.

Abraham Lincoln

Seek not the favour of the multitude; it is seldom got by honest and lawful means. But seek the testimony of few; and number not voices, but weigh them.

Immanuel Kant

There are no strangers here; only
friends you haven't yet met.

William Butler Yeats

Each friend represents a world in us,
a world possibly not born until they
arrive, and it is only by this meeting
that a new world is born.

Anais Nin

Love is the only force capable of
transforming an enemy into a friend.

Martin Luther King, Jr.

No friendship is an accident.

O. Henry

We must reach out our hand in friendship and dignity both to those who would befriend us and those who would be our enemy.

Arthur Ashe

He who sows courtesy reaps friendship,
and he who plants kindness gathers love.

Saint Basil

10 Ways To Make New Friends

- Ask questions – and listen to the answers!
- Smile and maintain eye contact
- Open up
- Be honest
- Be yourself
- Make the first move
- Keep in touch
- Meet in person
- Make an effort
- Say yes!

Life is partly what we make it, and partly
what it is made by the friends we choose.

Tennessee Williams

Of all the means to ensure happiness throughout the whole life, by far the most important is the acquisition of friends.

Epicurus

Be slow in choosing a friend,
slower in changing.

Benjamin Franklin

Sometimes friends begin as enemies,
and enemies begin as friends.

Levi Miller, *Pan* (2015)

Of all the things that are beyond my power, I value nothing more highly than to be allowed the honour of entering into bonds of friendship with people who sincerely love truth.

Baruch Spinoza

Be courteous to all, but intimate
with few, and let those few be well tried
before you give them your confidence.

George Washington

Friendships are discovered
rather than made.

Harriet Beecher Stowe

I know, first hand, that soccer brings
people together – all it takes is a ball
and a few people, and the seeds of
friendship are planted.

Ali Krieger

The best time to make friends is
before you need them.

Ethel Barrymore

Do I not destroy my enemies when
I make them my friends.

Abraham Lincoln

A friend may be waiting behind
a stranger's face.

Maya Angelou

Since there is nothing so well worth
having as friends, never lose a chance
to make them.

Francesco Guicciardini

Every new friend is a new adventure...
the start of more memories.

Patrick Lindsay

Don't make friends who are comfortable
to be with. Make friends who will force
you to lever yourself up.

Thomas J. Watson

We hate some persons because we do
not know them; and will not know them
because we hate them.

Charles Caleb Colton

Friendship is born at that moment when one person says to another, 'What! You too? I thought I was the only one.'

C.S. Lewis

Words are easy, like the wind; Faithful
friends are hard to find.

William Shakespeare

CHAPTER
3

A FRIEND IN NEED...

In this day and age it's
sometimes hard to know who
your real friends are.
Here are some wise words
to help you find out.

Friends show their love in times of trouble, not in happiness.

Euripides

The best friend is the man who in wishing
me well wishes it for my sake.

Aristotle

A friend is someone who knows all about you and still loves you.

Elbert Hubbard

My two best girlfriends are from secondary school. I don't have to explain anything to them. I don't have to apologize for anything. They know.

Emma Watson

A real friend is one who walks in when
the rest of the world walks out.

Walter Winchell

My definition of a friend is somebody who adores you even though they know the things you're most ashamed of.

Jodie Foster

Experts on romance say for a happy marriage there has to be more than a passionate love. For a lasting union, they insist, there must be a genuine liking for each other ...

... which, in my book, is a good definition for friendship.

Marilyn Monroe

You find out who your real friends are
when you're involved in a scandal.

Elizabeth Taylor

Love is blind. Friendship tries not to notice.

Angela Kendrick

Friendship is the hardest thing in the world to explain. It's not something you learn in school. But if you haven't learned the meaning of friendship, you really haven't learned anything.

Muhammad Ali

Friendship consists in forgetting
what one gives and remembering
what one receives.

Alexander Dumas

Friendship is one mind in two bodies.

Mencius

Love is flower-like; Friendship is a sheltering tree.

Samuel Taylor Coleridge

Real friendship, like real poetry, is
extremely rare – and precious as a pearl.

Tahar Ben Jelloun

BEST MOVIES ABOUT FRIENDSHIP

The Breakfast Club (1985)
Stand by Me (1986)
Thelma & Louise (1991)
Beaches (1988)
Fried Green Tomatoes (1991)
I Love You, Man (2009)
The Shawshank Redemption (1994)
Bridesmaids (2011)
50/50 (2011)
Mean Girls (2004)
Good Will Hunting (1998)

A friend is a beloved mystery; dearest always because he is not ourself, and has something in him which it is impossible for us to fathom. If it were not so, friendship would lose its chief zest.

Lucy Larcom

True friendship ought never to
conceal what it thinks.

Saint Jerome

True friendship comes when the silence
between two people is comfortable.

David Tyson

There are no rules for friendship.
It must be left to itself.

William Hazlitt

The worst part of success is trying to find someone who is happy for you.

Bette Midler

True friends are like diamonds – bright,
beautiful, valuable and always in style.

Nicole Richie

A true friend unbosoms freely, advises
justly, assists readily, adventures boldly,
takes all patiently, defends courageously,
and continues a friend unchangeably.

William Penn

Friendship is essentially a partnership.

Aristotle

A man's friendships are one of the
best measures of his worth.

Charles Darwin

Perhaps the most delightful friendships
are those in which there is much
agreement, much disputation, and yet
more personal liking.

George Eliot

Friendship is the finest balm for
the pangs of despised love.

Jane Austen

What do we live for, if it is not to make life less difficult for each other.

George Eliot

At the shrine of friendship never say die,
let the wine of friendship never run dry.

Victor Hugo

BEST SONGS TO SING WITH YOUR FRIENDS

"I'll Be There For You" – The Rembrandts

"You've Got a Friend" – James Taylor

"Lean on Me" – Bill Withers

"With a Little Help From My Friends"
– The Beatles

"You're My Best Friend" – Queen

"Wannabe" – The Spice Girls

"Ain't No Mountain High Enough" – Marvin
Gaye & Tammi Terrell

"We're Going to Be Friends"
– The White Stripes

"Bridge over Troubled Water"
– Simon & Garfunkel

"You Got a Friend in Me" – Randy Newman

There can be no friendship
without confidence, and no
confidence without integrity.

Samuel Johnson

True friendship is a plant of slow
growth, and must undergo and withstand
the shocks of adversity, before it is entitled
to the appellation.

George Washington

Lots of people want to ride with you in the limo, but what you want is someone who will take the bus with you when the limo breaks down.

Oprah Winfrey

All love that has not friendship for its base,
is like a mansion built upon the sand.

Ella Wheeler Wilcox

Marriage is the highest state of friendship. If happy, it lessens our cares by dividing them, at the same time that it doubles our pleasures by mutual participation.

Samuel Richardson

There is nothing I would not do for
those who are really my friends. I have
no notion of loving people by halves,
it is not my nature.

Jane Austen

The best part about having true friends
is that you can go months without seeing
them and they'll still be there for you and
act as if you'd never left.

Ariana Grande

It's the friends you can call up
at 4 a.m. that matter.

Marlene Dietrich

The ideal friendship is to feel as
one while remaining two.

Sophie Swetchine

There is nothing better than a friend,
unless it is a friend with chocolate.

Linda Grayson

CHAPTER
4

BFFs

There's nothing so precious
as a best friend, except perhaps
an old friend.

Age appears best in four things:
old wood to burn, old wine to drink, old
friends to trust and old authors to read.

Sir Francis Bacon

I cannot even imagine where I would be today were it not for that handful of friends who have given me a heart full of joy.

Charles R. Swindoll

BF: BEST FRIEND

BFF: BEST FRIENDS FOREVER

BFFEL: BEST FRIENDS FOR
EVERLASTING LIFE

FTTE: FRIENDS TILL THE END

TPIAP: TWO PEAS IN A POD

Man's best support is a very dear friend.

Cicero

The process of falling in love at first sight is as final as it is swift in such a case, but the growth of true friendship may be a lifelong affair.

Sarah Orne Jewett

A friend is one that knows you as you are, understands where you have been, accepts what you have become, and still, gently allows you to grow.

Unknown

The best way to mend a broken heart is time and girlfriends.

Gwyneth Paltrow

There is no enjoying the possession
of anything valuable unless one has
someone to share it with.

Seneca

There's not a word yet for old friends who've just met.

Jim Henson

No road is too long in the company
of a good friend.

Japanese proverb

I don't know what I would have done so many times in my life if I hadn't had my girlfriends.

Reese Witherspoon

One loyal friend is worth
ten thousand relatives.

Euripides

No one is useless in this world who
lightens the burdens of another.

Charles Dickens

You only meet your once-in-a-lifetime
friends...once in a lifetime.

Stymie, *The Little Rascals* (1994)

Some people go to priests.
Others to poetry. I to my friends.

Virginia Woolf

The best mirror is an old friend.

George Herbert

He will never have true friends who is afraid of making enemies.

William Hazlitt

FAMOUS TV BESTIES

Blair and Serena (*Gossip Girl*)

Rory and Lane (*Gilmore Girls*)

Seth and Ryan (*The OC*)

Cory and Shawn (*Boy Meets World*)

Meredith and Cristina (*Grey's Anatomy*)

Joey and Chandler (*Friends*)

Will and Grace (*Will & Grace*)

J.D. and Turk (*Scrubs*)

Scott and Stiles (*Teen Wolf*)

Sherlock and Watson (*Sherlock*)

We come from homes far from perfect, so you end up almost parent and sibling to your friends – your own chosen family. There's nothing like a really loyal, dependable, good friend. Nothing.

Jennifer Aniston

True friendship can afford true knowledge. It does not depend on darkness and ignorance.

Henry David Thoreau

No matter how tired I am,
I get dinner at least once a week with
my girlfriends. Or have a sleepover.
Otherwise my life is just all work.

Jennifer Lawrence

True friendship can afford true
knowledge. It does not depend on
darkness and ignorance.

Henry David Thoreau

As iron sharpens iron, so a friend
sharpens a friend.

King Solomon

Louie, I think this is the beginning of a
beautiful friendship.

Rick Blaine, *Casablanca* (1942)

Look, whatever happens, I'll always be there for you and you're never in this life on your own against the world ...

... you've always got a mate looking
out for you.

Declan Donnelly

Alone, bad. Friend, good.

The Monster, *Bride of Frankenstein* (1935)

Truth springs from argument
amongst friends.

David Hume

I found out what the secret to life is: friends. Best friends.

Ninny Threadgoode, *Fried Green Tomatoes* (1992)

It's an insane world but in it there
is one sanity: the loyalty of old friends.

Ben Hur

A boy's best friend is his mother.

Norman Bates, *Psycho* (1960)

There is no friendship, no love,
like that of the mother for the child.

Henry Ward Beecher

CHAPTER
5

KEEP YOUR FRIENDS CLOSE

Like anything worth having,
friendships often require some work
if they are to stand the test of time.
Making friends can be easy – holding
on to them is much harder.

Friendship is like money:
easier made than kept.

Samuel Butler

Don't walk behind me; I may not lead.
Don't walk in front of me; I may not follow.
Just walk beside me and be my friend.

Albert Camus

I never considered a difference of opinion in politics, in religion, in philosophy, as cause for withdrawing from a friend.

Thomas Jefferson

It is easier to forgive an enemy
than to forgive a friend.

William Blake

A quarrel between friends, when made up, adds a new tie to friendship.

Saint Francis de Sales

Never leave a friend behind. Friends
are all we have to get us through this
life – and they are the only things
from this world that we could
hope to see in the next.

Dean Koontz

It takes a great deal of bravery
to stand up to your enemies, but
a great deal more to stand up to
your friends.

Dumbledore,
Harry Potter and the Philosopher's Stone
(2001)

The most beautiful discovery true
friends make is that they can grow
separately without growing apart.

Elisabeth Foley

To throw away an honest friend is, as it were, to throw your life away.

Sophocles

I would rather walk with a friend in the dark, than alone in the light.

Helen Keller

The best thing to hold on to
in life is each other.

Arthur Schopenhauer

It is more shameful to distrust our friends than to be deceived by them.

Confucius

Friends are proved by adversity.

Cicero

I don't know how much longer I can keep going without a friend. I used to be able to do it very easily, but that was before I knew what having a friend was like.

Charlie, *The Perks of Being a Wallflower* (2012)

Keep your friends close,
and your enemies closer.

Sun Zhu, *The Art of War*

Friendship may, and often does,
grow into love, but love never
subsides into friendship.

Lord Byron

Friendship is not always the
sequel of obligation.

Samuel Johnson

There is no friendship that cares
about an overheard secret.

Alexandre Dumas

'Stay' is a charming word
in a friend's vocabulary.

Louisa May Alcott

To the world you may be just one person,
but to one person you may be the world.

Dr. Seuss

The shifts of fortune test the
reliability of friends.

Cicero

Time doesn't take away from
friendship, nor does separation.

Tennessee Williams

A friend to all is a friend to none.

Aristotle

Friendship is a pretty full-time occupation
if you really are friendly with somebody.
You can't have too many friends because
then you're just not really friends.

Truman Capote

I was tired of pretending that
I was someone else just to get
along with people just for the
sake of having friendships.

Kurt Cobain

Dear George, remember no man is a
failure who has friends.

Clarence Oddbody, *It's a Wonderful Life* **(1946)**

CHAPTER
6

YOU'VE GOT A FRIEND

There's nothing so painful as the loss of a treasured companion. Peruse these words of wisdom at times when, for whatever reason, friends feel few and far between.

Be a friend to thyself, and
others will be so too.

Thomas Fuller

Share your smile with the world.
It's a symbol of friendship and peace.

Christie Brinkley

A single rose can be my garden ...
a single friend, my world.

Leo Buscaglia

My books are friends that never fail me.

Thomas Carlyle

The language of friendship is not
words but meanings.

Henry David Thoreau

For beautiful eyes, look for the good in others; for beautiful lips, speak only words of kindness; and for poise, walk with the knowledge that you are never alone.

Audrey Hepburn

Find a group of people who challenge
and inspire you; spend a lot of time with
them, and it will change your life.

Amy Poehler

When the world is so complicated,
the simple gift of friendship is within
all of our hands.

Maria Shriver

True friendship is like sound health; the
value of it is seldom known until it is lost.

Charles Caleb Colton

No distance of place or lapse of time
can lessen the friendship of those
who are thoroughly persuaded of
each other's worth.

Robert Southey

They may forget what you said, but they will never forget how you made them feel.

Carl W. Buechner

Associate yourself with people of
good quality, for it is better to be
alone than in bad company.

Booker T. Washington

A friend is a gift you give yourself.

Robert Louis Stevenson

Sweet is the memory of distant friends.

Washington Irving

If ever there is tomorrow when we're not together ... there is something you must always remember. You are braver than you believe, stronger than you seem, and smarter than you think ...

... but the most important thing is, even if we're apart... I'll always be with you.

Winnie-the-Pooh

The only way to have a friend is to be one.

Ralph Waldo Emerson